For more inspiration, get the book!

YOU MIGHT DIE TOMORROW

SO LIVE TODAY

FACE YOUR FEAR OF DEATH TO LIVE YOUR MOST MEANINGFUL LIFE

KATE MANSER

Available at www.katemanser.com/books
& Amazon, Barnes & Noble, Audible, Hoopla, Bookshop.org

HIGHLINE
HOUSE

THE ALIVE WORKBOOK.

Copyright © 2022 by Kate Manser. All rights reserved.

Published by Highline House Publishing.

Cover and interior designed by Marija Stojkovic at Awaken Entrepreneur.
Paperback ISBN: 978-1-952018-04-6 | Ebook ISBN: 978-1-952018-05-3

For all the people who love
Dan Fredinburg.

Table of Contents

Introduction	06
What Not to Do	08
The Deathbed Gut Check	17
The Deathbed Meditation	22
The Delta Assessment	28
Big & Small Meaningful Things Journal	34
THE ALIVE YEAR - 52 Meaningful Things Challenge	38
Forgive & Be Free	45
I Feel So ALIVE	51
Hack Your Fear of Death	52
Closing: Do Meaningful Stuff & Start Now	53

> **If you're reading this...**
> Congratulations, you're alive. If that's not something to smile about, then I don't know what is.
>
> Chad W. Sugg

Introduction

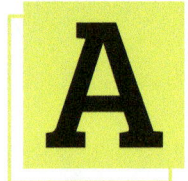round age thirty, having architected my life following the blueprint of my unconscious self, I looked around and thought, "Where the hell am I?"

I had spent years climbing the mountain peaks of high school, college, marriage, dog, job, and then *another* dog...and I realized I was on the wrong mountain. I realized I hadn't even consciously chosen to climb this mountain, Mount Societal Blueprint. I had just done it because...well, I wasn't exactly sure why.

My radical awakening came when I realized I wanted to really live before I die, that it could happen tomorrow, and that I am in full control of how I live until that mystery moment comes. My realization and acceptance that I might die tomorrow transformed me from a person who felt my life was happening to me as I sat lost, unfulfilled, and wistful into a person who lives in alignment with my personal meaning, vibrant with the urgency to really live and really be me.

On the many days since that realization when I fall back into apathy, overwhelm, and fear, I pull from my pocket my free source of radical perspective and motivation: that I will die and I don't know when.

I have spent years researching the psychological, philosophical, historical, and anecdotal perspectives and experiences on how thinking about your death reminds you to live. It turns out that everyone from Plato to Buddha to Tim McGraw have proclaimed the value of living with an awareness of the reality of death.

But death is death -- what we have in the palm of our hand now is life. The purpose of this workbook is to shift you from passenger of your life to wind-in-your-hair driver. It's engineered so that if you complete it, you will be crushing future regret, living immediately, and letting your true self shine brighter than you ever have before. You will be living vibrantly with gratitude and joy. You will release darkness, repair relationships, and live in alignment with your vision of *your* most meaningful life.

You can do this workbook in the order it is presented or in the order you prefer. The chapter start pages with inspiring quotes are also coloring pages! Take it slow and do the LIVE NOW challenges. They are full of adventure, peace, and fulfillment. Don't be shy -- share your experience with these challenges and inspiration with your family and friends so you can inspire them to live their most meaningful lives, too.

I have written this book to inspire you, reader, to live a vibrant and awake life you couldn't possibly regret. To help you love yourself enough that you can't be anything but an expression of love and light to everyone you meet. To push you to stop wasting your life and start living like the badass you are.

Many people who are faced with imminent death -- through terminal illness, a near-death experience, or have grappled with loved ones dying -- have experienced a radical shift in life perspective, a chance to look at their lives with clear eyes and an open heart. But why should tragedy be a prerequisite to appreciating life and living vibrantly? It's not. **Remembering you might die tomorrow could save your life. Start now.**

It is not death that a man should fear, but he should fear

NEVER BEGINNING TO LIVE.

Marcus Aurelius

WHAT NOT TO DO - Regrets of the Dying

The most common regrets of people at the end of their lives are, for the living, a guide on how *not* to live. The people on their deathbed have an advantage: perspective. But you, alive one, also have an advantage: time.

If you're still not quite sure what to start doing to live your most meaningful life, perhaps you can instead focus on *not* doing the stuff that's bringing you down and out of alignment.

REGRET #1: I wish I'd had the courage to live a life true to myself, not the life others expected of me.

1. List some thing(s) you have done throughout your life to appease or impress your parents, family, employer, or friends.

2. MANTRA: I am alive to shine. Write it 5 times!

⚡ LIVE NOW: Go on your preferred social media platform now and unfollow 10 (or more) accounts that make you feel bad about your body, lifestyle, or income.

The Alive *Workbook* 012

WHAT NOT TO DO - *Regrets of the Dying*

3. Name a celebrity or someone you know personally who totally marches to the beat of their own drummer / is so weird and awesome.

⚡ LIVE NOW: Next time you're debating wearing that kinda weird outfit, speaking in front of others, or telling people about your unique hobby - think of this person and do it!

REGRET #2: I wish I hadn't worked so hard.

1. Does your job drain your soul? If yes, Why? Circle all that apply.

   a. I think my company does more harm in the world than good.

   b. This work is not well suited for my strengths.

   c. I have a bad attitude toward this job / work in general.

   d. I don't like the people I work with.

   e. I really wish I was doing this kind of work instead: _____

   f. Other:

WHAT NOT TO DO - *Regrets of the Dying*

2. If your job drains your soul, why are you still in it?

3. Do the above reasons hold up when you play out The Deathbed Gut Check against them? Why or why not?

4. What part(s) of your job do you find meaningful?
   → If you can't think of anything, *everyone* can find meaning in being a source of positive energy for the people you work with.

5. Journal on your job / career & living in alignment with your meaning. What can you do to bring more meaning to your work life? Should you change careers? What's holding you back?

WHAT NOT TO DO - *Regrets of the Dying*

REGRET #3: I wish I'd had the courage to express my feelings.

1. Do I often suppress my true personality, essence, and emotions? Be honest. If yes, write down your fears / why you hold back.

⚡ LIVE NOW: Resolve in this moment now to NOT suppress yourself next time you feel the urge to hold back, be quiet, shrink, or put on a false mask. Write down a mantra to reflect your courageous resolve to be yourself & shine brightly:

WHAT NOT TO DO - *Regrets of the Dying*

REGRET #4: I wish I'd stayed in touch with my friends.

⚡ LIVE NOW: Write the names of three people in your life whom you value but don't see or keep in close contact with. Then choose a random date of the year that is NOT their birthday. This is now your annual "Call _____ and tell them that you love them day." Add it as a repeating annual event on your online calendar.

Name	Their "Random" Date
_____	_____
_____	_____
_____	_____
_____	_____
_____	_____
_____	_____
_____	_____

Even just ONE day per year to reach out is enough to keep a friendship nurtured, and who knows - maybe this one day will blossom into more days of connection & love.

WHAT NOT TO DO - *Regrets of the Dying*

REGRET #5: I wish I'd let myself be happier.

Journal / brainstorm on the areas of your life you take too seriously and how you could loosen up & enjoy more.

WORK

FAMILY

HOBBIES

WHAT NOT TO DO - *Regrets of the Dying*

ADVENTURE

HEALTH

OTHER

YOU KNOW THE TRUTH BY THE WAY IT FEELS

THE DEATHBED Gut Check

Use the impermanent nature of life -- the fact that it could all end tomorrow -- to dissolve the layers of confusing muck from your decisions: insignificant worries, the expectations' of others, ego-driven beliefs, and the notion that we'll always have more time to do stuff.

What will be revealed is your sparkling and meaningful Best Path.

How it Works

- Consider a choice in your life now — perhaps a job change, a geographical move, or whether to repair or dismantle a relationship.

- Now imagine yourself on your deathbed looking back on the path you chose (which, in the present, is an option you are weighing).

- Observe how you feel in your gut.

I call this 'The Deathbed Gut Check.' I use it to check in with my Truest Self in everyday scenarios and to make the big decisions of my life. It's given me so much clarity on how I truly want to live and motivation to act sooner rather than later. Now it's your turn

Deathbed Gut Check Practice

Consider a choice you are trying to make in your life in the present but feel decision paralysis between options.

Examples:
Should I quit this job?
Should I tell her that I love her?
Should I give this business idea a try?
Should I make this big purchase?

The choice I am struggling with is: _____

Now with this decision in mind, imagine yourself in the future on your deathbed, looking back at your life. Imagine yourself looking back at yourself having NOT done the thing you are considering. Close your eyes and imagine this. You may want to first imagine yourself on your deathbed. In your mind, create the scene of the room you're in and the bed you lie in. You're at the end of your life and you settle back for a life review. Play the tape of your life review "movie" with how things might go and how you might feel if you don't do the action you're considering.

How do you feel looking back on your life with that thing left undone?

- How do you feel in your gut and body? Do you feel a tightness or a lightness in your gut? Do you feel happy or tired?

- How do you feel emotionally? Do you feel sadness creeping up or do you feel a sense of pride?

I feel:
(list or write out your feelings)

THE DEATHBED *Gut Check*

You may want to now repeat The Deathbed Gut Check as you did above, but this time observe your feelings as you look back on your life having DONE the thing you are considering. Play the tape of how your life might have gone if you make the change / do the thing.

How do you feel looking back on your life having done that thing you are considering?

I feel:
(list or write out your feelings)

You can also use The Deathbed Gut check to determine how important something is to you.

Think of something you have been putting off in your life. Perhaps a hobby like painting or running.

OR

Think about something you've considered doing but aren't sure you want in life, like getting married or having children.

Do The Deathbed Gut Check for that thing, then check your feelings on it:

Ask yourself: How do you feel on your deathbed having NOT done that while you were alive?

I feel:
(list or write out your feelings)

The Alive *Workbook*

THE DEATHBED *Gut Check*

==You can also use The Deathbed Gut Check to weigh your behavior. Think of something you have been doing that makes you feel secretly guilty.==

Examples: drinking too much alcohol, ignoring your neighbors, not calling / spending time with a family member

Do The Deathbed Gut Check.
Consider how you will feel on your deathbed if you don't change this behavior.

I feel:
(list or write out your feelings)

Now that you have become familiar with The Deathbed Gut Check in its longer form, apply The Deathbed Gut Check in your daily life. Next time you're faced with a decision (whether to go to that party, whether to call in sick to work, whether to call that person back now or later), condense The Deathbed Gut Check down to a 30 second meditation, then a 10-second meditation, and eventually you will be able to face a decision, imagine yourself on your deathbed looking back at your choice, and make your Best Path decision in 5-seconds on the fly!

I am of the nature to grow old;
I am of the nature to sicken;
I am of the nature to die.

 **Buddha**

THE DEATHBED Meditation

The Deathbed Gut Check is awesome for making big life decisions and for daily split decisions, but sometimes you need to zoom out even further to get maximum perspective on your life.

This is why I created The Deathbed Meditation.

Meditating on mortality, decay, and the end of one's existence is an ancient practice. Monks, Stoics, and just about every major religion has a history of mortality awareness ritual. With my Deathbed Meditation, the age-old benefits of mortality contemplation are fused with a powerful life review to make you more open to your own future dying experience and impart radical perspective on your past, present, and future life.

Listen to The Deathbed Meditation at www.youmightdietomorrow.com/deathbed-meditation and then use these pages to reflect on your experiences and insights.

Journal Questions for after The Deathbed Meditation

Your deathbed visualization
- Describe the deathbed scene you envisioned. Where was it? What did you notice about it? How did it make you feel?

THE DEATHBED *Meditation*

Your life review

Relationships
- Write the names of the people who came up when you considered who is truly important and meaningful to you. Who you feel most connected to and truly love?

```
┌─────────────────────────────────────────────────────────┐
│                                                         │
│                                                         │
│                                                         │
└─────────────────────────────────────────────────────────┘
```

Now circle the names of who you would like to do a better job of expressing and showing your love and care to.

⚡ LIVE NOW: Text each one of those people out of the blue, "I really love you" or something caring RIGHT NOW.

- Who from your past that you have lost touch with would you like to reconnect with?

```
┌─────────────────────────────────────────────────────────┐
│                                                         │
│                                                         │
│                                                         │
└─────────────────────────────────────────────────────────┘
```

⚡ LIVE NOW: Write them an email, text, or call them. Right now!
Turn to the bottom of page 109 of the book for an idea of what to write or say.

The Alive *Workbook*

THE DEATHBED *Meditation*

- Write the name(s) of who you need to forgive to release negativity from your spirit before you die.

[   ]

- Write the name(s) of who you can apologize to for wrongdoing.

[   ]

⚡ LIVE NOW: Turn to page 45 to make it right by writing a forgiveness and/or amends letter(s).

THE DEATHBED *Meditation*

Meaningful Actions

- What is a dream or goal you have that you have put off -- but if you were given six months or 1 year to live, you would start immediately?

```
┌─────────────────────────────────────────────────────────────────────┐
│                                                                     │
│                                                                     │
│                                                                     │
│                                                                     │
└─────────────────────────────────────────────────────────────────────┘
```

- What's something you spend too much time on that depletes your energy, doesn't bring you much meaning, and makes you feel darker or heavier?

```
┌─────────────────────────────────────────────────────────────────────┐
│                                                                     │
│                                                                     │
│                                                                     │
│                                                                     │
└─────────────────────────────────────────────────────────────────────┘
```

- What is an activity that brings you joy, lights you up, makes you feel light & free?

```
┌─────────────────────────────────────────────────────────────────────┐
│                                                                     │
│                                                                     │
│                                                                     │
│                                                                     │
└─────────────────────────────────────────────────────────────────────┘
```

- List adjectives and/or colors or draw doodles to represent your **mindset and attitude towards life prior to the meditation / up to now:**

- Now, list adjectives and/or colors or draw doodles to represent how you want your **mindset and attitude towards life to be <u>from here on out</u>:**

Every day is a "bonus" day. I wake up most mornings and blink in disbelief that I got to wake up *again* and enjoy this incredible life. Every day is a new chance to do things differently, to choose joy, and to slow down to truly experience the wonder of being alive.

Now go, BE ALIVE!

THE DELTA ASSESSMENT

There is a lot going on in life. We get pulled in so many different directions! It feels like there are so many competing priorities!

Don't you just feel exhausted sometimes? Like, how does anyone keep their head above water?

You need The Delta Assessment - not just today but a few times throughout the year.

The Delta Assessment achieves 3 benefits:

1. It outlines the key aspects of life which we divide our time and energy between, giving you a bird's eye view of all the moving parts of life.
2. It helps you rank all of those moving parts according to what really matters to you and what's just not a priority.
3. It helps you discover where you are overspending and underspending your time and energy in relation to your true priorities so you can adjust to live your most meaningful life.

Do The Delta Assessment now, and again every 3-6 months.

Instructions

In my book, I recommend that you do each column separately:

1. First, assign an Importance value to every line in the Importance Rating column.
2. Then, assign an Expenditure rating to every line in the Expenditure Rating column.
3. Finally, subtract your Expenditure Rating from your Importance rating to discover where you have the greatest Delta between what matters and how you actually live.

However, you can also analyze line by line if you prefer.

1. Starting with Spouse/partner/romantic love, assess your Importance Rating.
2. Then move to Expenditure Rating and assess your Time & Energy Expenditure for Spouse/partner/romantic love.
3. Finally, subtract your Expenditure Rating from your Importance rating to discover where you have the greatest Delta between what matters and how you actually live.
4. Repeat for each line.

THE DELTA Assessment

	Importance rating How important is each of these aspects to you and your life? 1=not at all important; 10=profoundly important	**Expenditure rating** How much time and energy do you expend on each of these aspects? 1=no energy at all; 10=significant time/energy	**THE DELTA** Subtract Column 2 from Column 1 to discover the greatest deltas between your meaning and how you actually live.
Spouse/partner/romantic love			
Family of Origin (parents, siblings)			
Children			
Friends			
Earning money			
Work/Career Achievement			
Service & helping others			
Quiet time / meditation / calm reflection			
Enjoying Your Life eg. vacation, hobbies, "just for fun"			
Being outside in nature			
Learning / Growth Self-improvement			
Creating/Expressing eg. writing/ journaling, singing, art			
Physical wellness eg. exercise, sleep, stretching			
(optional: add your own)			

THE DELTA Assessment

 LIVE NOW: Imagine you're going to die in 1 year. Now complete The Delta Assessment again from that perspective.

	Importance rating How important is each of these aspects to you and your life? 1=not at all important; 10=profoundly important	**Expenditure rating** How much time and energy do you expend on each of these aspects? 1=no energy at all; 10=significant time/ energy	**THE DELTA** Subtract Column 2 from Column 1 to discover the greatest deltas between your meaning and how you actually live.
Spouse/partner/ romantic love			
Family of Origin (parents, siblings)			
Children			
Friends			
Earning money			
Work/Career Achievement			
Service & helping others			
Quiet time / meditation / calm reflection			
Enjoying Your Life eg. vacation, hobbies, "just for fun"			
Being outside in nature			
Learning / Growth Self-improvement			
Creating/Expressing eg. writing/ journaling, singing, art			
Physical wellness eg. exercise, sleep, stretching			
(optional: add your own)			

THE DELTA Assessment

	Importance rating How important is each of these aspects to you and your life? 1=not at all important; 10=profoundly important	**Expenditure rating** How much time and energy do you expend on each of these aspects? 1=no energy at all; 10=significant time/energy	**THE DELTA** Subtract Column 2 from Column 1 to discover the greatest deltas between your meaning and how you actually live.
Spouse/partner/ romantic love			
Family of Origin (parents, siblings)			
Children			
Friends			
Earning money			
Work/Career Achievement			
Service & helping others			
Quiet time / meditation / calm reflection			
Enjoying Your Life eg. vacation, hobbies, "just for fun"			
Being outside in nature			
Learning / Growth Self-improvement			
Creating/Expressing eg. writing/ journaling, singing, art			
Physical wellness eg. exercise, sleep, stretching			
(optional: add your own)			

Reflect on Your Results

What are the 3 areas with the greatest delta between how you spend your time and what's important to you?

1. _____
2. _____
3. _____

What are you doing well? What are the 3 areas where you're most in alignment (have the lowest delta number)?

1. _____
2. _____
3. _____

What can you do to spend less time on the activities you're overinvesting into?

What can you adjust in your life to spend more time on that stuff you really care about?

Note to Self: None of us are getting out of here alive, so please stop treating yourself like an after thought. Eat the delicious food. Walk in the sunshine. Jump in the ocean. Say the truth that you're carrying in your heart like hidden treasure. Be silly. Be kind. Be weird. There's no time for anything else.

Nanea Hoffman

BIG & SMALL MEANINGFUL THINGS JOURNAL

If you know you want to live meaningfully, but don't know where to start, let's break it down. I look at creating meaning in my life in two main categories: Big Meaningful Things and Small Meaningful Things.

Big Meaningful Things are landmark, "bucket list"-type life dreams and ventures. We usually only do these once or a few times in life. They're big, exhilarating, often risky, and regardless of the outcome, we usually feel fulfilled just to have taken the chance to do them! Examples include a career change, having kid(s), moving to a new state or country, donating an organ, starting a nonprofit, going skydiving, choosing a long-term partner, taking a big trip, and making big lifestyle changes like quitting alcohol or starting exercise.

Small Meaningful Things are everyday acts -- and also our daily mindset choices.

Our mindset choices are unique in that they're usually both an overarching value choice ("I choose to be a kind & loving person") and they're also micro-choices in the moment ("I choose to respond to the person who verbally lashed out on me with compassion and patience"). Meaningful mindset choices include waking up every day with gratitude for life, approaching your day with zeal and fun instead of being overly serious, choosing respond to a frustrating person or situation with compassion instead of anger, seeing the good in others, and valuing time over money.

In addition to the mindset we choose to approach our life, we can also take action in small ways every day to lead a fulfilling life. Everyday meaningful actions are our decisions on how to spend our Life Time and Energy that are in alignment with living our own version of a good life. Some examples include spending time with people you love, pausing to enjoy the sunset, donating your time each week or month to a nonprofit, meditating, chatting warmly with strangers, and taking time to enjoy your hobbies.

Both Big and Small Meaningful Things require inspired action on your part to make happen! There is lots of potential for crossover, too -- maybe you start an everyday practice of writing or journaling and it turns into a major part of your life or even a book. Or maybe what starts out as meditating for a few minutes every day becomes a central part of your life or even contributes to an awakening or realization that changes you forever.

The common thread in Big and Small Meaningful Things is intentionality and inspired action. Choose your best life and go for it! Mess up along the way, get back up, and keep living your best life while you're still alive. You'll have nothing to regret at the end.

On the next pages, dream, imagine, and set (for now!) your life dreams (the big meaningful things), the mindset you have in your ideal life, and the little everyday moments that make for your most fulfilling life. This is your roadmap for how to live each day like you might die tomorrow.

BIG & SMAIL *Meaningful Things Journal*

BIG MEANINGFUL THINGS

Draw/Doodle/Write

My big dreams, big goals, big meaningful actions & experiences for life.
What I want to do before I die. :)

BIG & SMALL *Meaningful Things Journal*

SMALL MEANINGFUL THINGS - MINDSET

Draw/doodle/write

Adjectives & images that represent the mindset with which I want to approach my life & how I want to be remembered after I'm gone. :)

BIG & SMALL *Meaningful Things Journal*

SMALL MEANINGFUL THINGS - ACTIONS

Draw/doodle/write

The everyday experiences, moments, & actions that will collectively make me feel that I have lived a joyful & fulfilled life. The small moments of life that make me feel alive. :)

THE ALIVE YEAR

52 Meaningful Things - 1 challenge per week for 1 full year that will change you, challenge you, and make you feel more alive than you have ever felt. BONUS: You living your most alive life will create a ripple effect of positivity that will spread to friends, family, and probably thousands of people you don't even know. This is your chance to change the world for the better. BE alive!

1. Bring your neighbor cookies. Bake 'em or buy 'em - doesn't matter. Just knock on their door, hand them the cookies, and say "Just wanted to bring you some cheer!"

2. Think of someone you know who is going through a hard time in life. Call them.
   Inspiration for what to say: "Hey, I'm just calling because I know sometimes life sucks but you should know that I care about you and I'm behind you even when I'm not around. Want to talk about what's going on?"

3. Text the people you care about most in life out of the blue, "I really love you" or something caring RIGHT NOW.
   Tip: Who did you write down on page 13?

4. Who are treasured friends from your past who you have lost touch with? Write them an email, text, or call them. Right now!
   Tip: In the YMDT book, turn to the bottom of page 109 to read what my friend Caroline wrote to me after we were out of touch for over a decade.

5. Go on your preferred social media platform now and unfollow 10 (or more) accounts that make you feel bad about your body, lifestyle, or income.

6. Wear a totally out of your comfort zone but fun (& maybe kinda weird) outfit today

7. Forgive someone & release yourself from negative energy. Write a forgiveness letter(s) to someone you hold anger toward.
   For inspiration, watch the documentary Surviving Dr. Mengele or look up the subject, Eva Kor & her inspiring path to forgiving the people who tortured she and her sister.

8. Make amends. Turn to page 49 to make it right by writing an amends letter(s) to someone whom you have hurt or wronged in the past.

9. Go for a slow, meditative walk focusing on the beauty of the world around you.

10. Next time you stub your toe, get cut off in traffic, or drop your toast, chuckle to yourself instead of getting mad. Force yourself to laugh and shake it off every time. Do this enough times and you will retrain your brain to react with humor instead of anger.

11. Smile at every stranger you see today.

12. Take a cold shower (or at minimum, finish your hot shower with a blast of cold water) to wake you up and condition your endurance! BONUS: Jump into a cold body of water like a spring or cold pool!

13. Take a portrait photo of the six people closest to you. Try to bring out their natural beauty and what you love about them.

14. Make a list of 10 things you are SO DONE with in life. And then actually be done with them. Let go!

15. Go on a hike you've never been on before.

16. Stop what you are doing every day for a week to take in the sunset.

17. Go to the store and buy six bouquets of flowers. Hand them out to random people.
    Tip: Whole Foods Market has great bouquets for $5!

18. Give someone an unexpected gift today.

19. Buy a pack of greeting cards & some stamps. Write heartfelt cards to people you care about…and actually mail them!

20. Write down every "divine inkling" you get this week. Every random idea or thought that you may normally forget about. Use that as inspiration for next week's challenges!

21. Buy a homeless person coffee & a breakfast sandwich. Chat with them while they eat it.

22. Go outside one night and look up at the stars for 60 minutes. No phone, no distractions, just you tripping out at the wonder of it all.

23. Paint or color an abstract piece -- let your color choices and brush/marker strokes flow.

24. Play a silly & good-natured prank on someone.
    Ideas: jump out and scare someone, put a rubber band on the sink sprayer, tap on the shoulder when they're not looking, call and act like they called you but you're busy.

25. Make a playlist of songs that instantly put you in a good mood when you hear them. Play it now and anytime you're feeling down or blah.

26. Ask & take someone on a proper date.

27. Stop watching television / streaming for 1 week. Make a plan for what you'll do instead to enrich your soul.

28. Meditate outside in nature. Activate each of your senses, one by one: listen -- really listen -- with every ounce of your being. Feel the sun on your back and the breeze on your cheek. Breathe in and focus on the scent and temperature of the air. Let yourself float way deeply into the present moment.

29. Donate an uncomfortable amount of money to the nonprofit organization of your choice. Can you donate 1% of your annual income? Either don't tell anyone, or rally others to donate as well.

30. Make a "playdate" with a kid. Call a friend who has a kid, your own kid, whoever - and for at least 60 minutes, go all-in on the imaginative world with that kid or kids. No distractions, no adulting (other than avoiding real danger), no real world stuff, just total imagination play & joy.

31. Beverage change week: switch from coffee to tea, tea to coffee, and/or abstain from alcohol for a week.

32. Write something and post it online. You probably know the thing you've already written that could speak to others. If not, write an essay about a challenge you've overcome recently - where you started, how the challenge came about, how you felt when faced with it, how you overcame it, and how you feel today. Post it to social media or medium.com.

33. Go camping somewhere in your own town.

34. Plant something. Nurture it. Sing it songs! Watch it grow.

35. Pick a "bad" habit or something you'd like to change in your life and dedicate this week to changing it. Hyperfocus on this 1 goal for this 1 week! Don't get distracted!

    What I'm focusing on stopping/starting/changing this week:
    _____

36. Give nonphysical compliments to people every day this week. Don't compliment their hair; instead let them know a personal trait you appreciate about them.

37. Meditate for 5 minutes every morning before you do anything else.

38. Release any feelings of "owing" your parents or childhood caretakers any aspect of your life other than gratitude. Resolve to live from here on out for fulfilling your joy & dreams, not theirs.

39. OFFLINE DAY. You know what to do. Phone off. Computer off. TV off. 24 hours: GO.

40. Stick your head out the window (or sunroof!) while in the car. At minimum, drive with the windows down & the tunes up.

41. Wake up & watch the sun rise in all its glory.

42. Think of something that scares you (spiders, heights, enclosed spaces). Seek it out and do your own exposure therapy.

43. Go pick up trash on the side of the road, the beach, your local hiking track. Don't get angry at the trash (or the people who dropped it)! Do it with love for Mother Earth and joy for the experience to be out in nature.

44. Dedicate this week to not comparing yourself to others. In its place, feel genuine goodwill & excitement for the gifts & accomplishments of others.

45. Take a bath or do something luxurious that has no other purpose than to make you feel great.

46. Do not talk about the weather or current events for an entire week. Fill the space with questions about dreams, life, feelings, jokes, whatever!

47. Buy a YOU MIGHT DIE TOMORROW t-shirt -- wear it and see what meaningful conversations & interactions you cultivate!

48. Chat with strangers you come across in your everyday life this week: in line, at work, on the phone with customer service. Ask them how their life is going or what makes them happiest.

49. Go outside and walk through the grass (or even on the sidewalk!) with no shoes on. Feel your connection to Mother Nature, Earth, and the great cycle of life.

50. Write a heartfelt note of appreciation to someone you admire but don't know.

51. Give at least $1 to every single fundraiser, homeless person, nonprofit that crosses your path this week, in person or online.

52. Go outside and lie down for at least 30 minutes. Be still and watch the clouds go by or the branches sway in the wind. Forget about your problems and focus in on the details of the clouds or the tree. Appreciate the beauty.

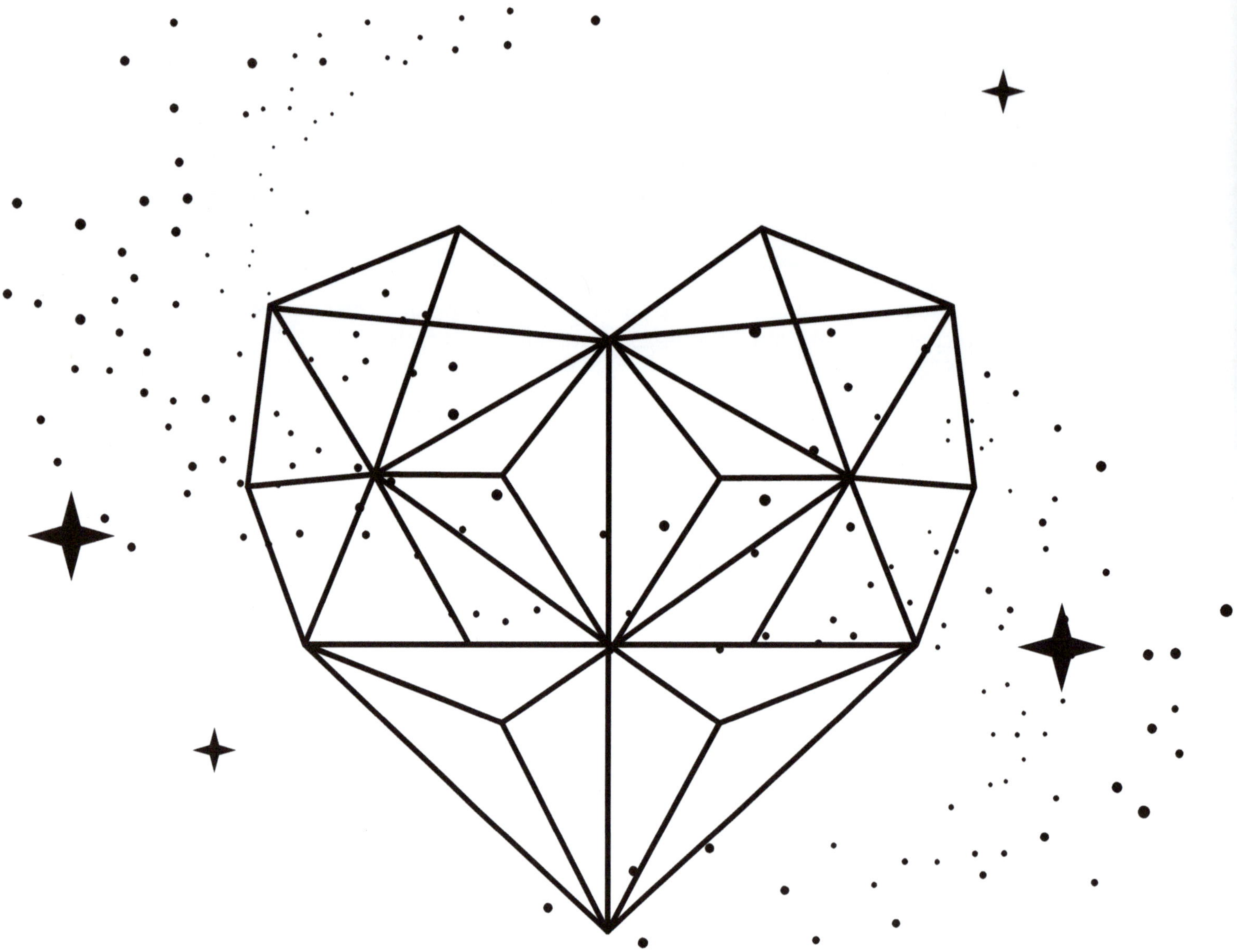

> Forgiveness is really nothing more than an act of self-healing and self-empowerment. I call it a miracle medicine. It is free, it works, and has no side effects.
>
> Eva Kor

FORGIVE AND BE FREE

Don't take your anger & resentments to the grave. Forgive now & free yourself to live lighter, brighter, & with inner peace.

For inspiration, watch the documentary Surviving Dr. Mengele or look up the subject, Eva Kor & her inspiring path to forgiving the people who tortured she and her sister. You can also read my story of resolving resentment toward my mom:

My experience resolving resentment:

Remember that every person is a soul on our own path. Here we are in this life, all just doing our best and inevitably mucking it up along the way.

I used to have so much anger toward my mom. She started drinking a lot when I was in high school and over the years I saw her go into a darker and darker state. I was so angry that she chose to go into oblivion instead of live her life! I was so angry that she couldn't muster the courage to face her inner demons and heal. I was so angry that she was wasting her precious life time and her beautiful soul to her own pain.

Then one day, I saw a scene illuminated in my mind. It was my mom at 21 years old when I was a baby. She was holding me so carefully against her chest. I looked up at her and I saw her for who she really was: a soul who had suffered profound trauma herself as a young woman and who walked down her life path to eventually give birth to me. She held me now with the best of intentions and with so much love, but she also brought to motherhood the collection of all of her life experiences, including her pain and trauma. I saw in her face pure love and I saw in her path her humanity; the messiness of the human condition. I saw her both as my mother, as a human, and as a soul. My anger evaporated and I accepted her for who she is. I accepted that her healing comes at her and her soul's pace, not my timeline. I realized that I cannot change her; all I can do is love her while we're both still alive.

***

P.S. Now that I have forgiven her, I can now see that all the times I tried to change her and treated her with disdain and anger actually requires that I make amends *to her*. More on amends in the next section.

My resentments:

Name	Why I am angry / hurt
_____	_____
_____	_____
_____	_____
_____	_____
_____	_____
_____	_____
_____	_____
_____	_____
_____	_____
_____	_____
_____	_____
_____	_____
_____	_____
_____	_____

Journal on How & Why You Will Forgive Those You Hold Resentment Toward

"

All streams flow to the ocean because it is lower than they are.

HUMILITY GIVES IT ITS POWER.

Lao Tzu

"

FORGIVE And Be Free

AMENDS - Leave Your Mistakes in the Here & Now

Clear your conscience. Lift the weight. Spread light. List the people to whom you owe an apology for your past behavior. Be honest & humble. Lay it all out!

Name	What I did that hurt or wronged this person
_____	_____
_____	_____
_____	_____
_____	_____
_____	_____
_____	_____
_____	_____
_____	_____
_____	_____
_____	_____
_____	_____

LIVE NOW:
Write your amends letter(s). Write your most important letters apologizing to the people you hurt or wronged in the past. Be brave and send the letter - expect no reply or forgiveness.

> **Worried about tomorrow, one cannot fully experience the wild beauty of today.**

Kate Manser

I FEEL SO ALIVE

List, doodle, write in big letters all the activities in life that make you feel the most ALIVE.

HACK YOUR FEAR OF DEATH

How to Hack Your Fear of Death to Live Your Most Meaningful Life

1. Acknowledge that death is scary

WRITE IT: Brain, Heart, & Soul dump of the aspects of death, dying, and mortality that scare you:

2. Cultivate a gentle awareness of mortality in your everyday life.

> ⚡ **LIVE NOW:**
> Close your eyes and imagine the Circle of Life and the grand cycles of Mother Nature...flowers blooming and drying out and then popping up next spring and repeating the cycle all over again. Generations coming and going over thousands of years. Let that visual flow wherever your heart takes it...

3. Actively live meaningfully.

You know what to do: All the stuff you have written about in this workbook! And the ALIVE Year!

CLOSING

Do Meaningful Stuff & Start Today

You've got this one life in this body and this set of circumstances. You have no idea how long you have to live. Don't wait until someone dies or you get cancer or you're on your deathbed to make the most of your alive time and do your Meaningful Things. This is your chance to live and shine and be the most you that you can be while you're still alive & kicking with breath in your chest and life coursing through your veins! Why not? What else are you gonna do? What's the point of it all if not to enjoy, do good, be love, and have fun? You might die tomorrow but by God, you have beautiful, ephemeral, stunning today. You can trudge through life as a martyr for your job or your kids or whatever or you can skip through as a beacon of love for your work, your family, and the world. The world needs you. I need you! Join me in my completely nonexclusive Grateful To Be Alive Club. It sure is a beautiful day to be alive, after all.

All my best and Happy Today!

Kate

"ADVENTURE AWAITS."

Dan Fredinburg

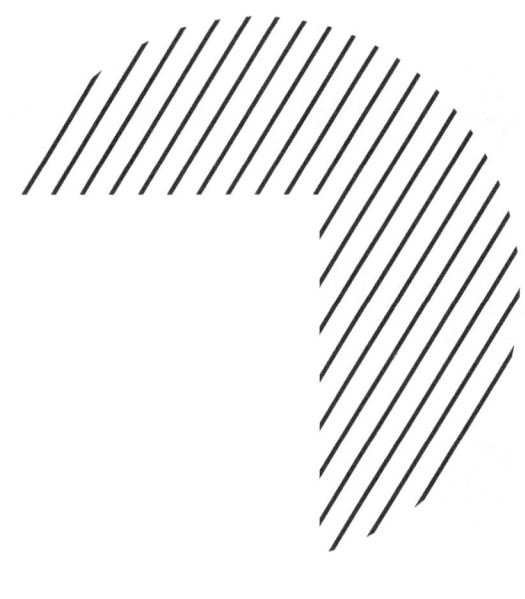

Follow Kate

◉ @thealivekate

𝗳 You Might Die Tomorrow

Get free weekly life brighteners

TEXT ALIVE to 512-898-7850

from Kate